Myths and Maxims

A Catalog of Superstitions, Spirits and Sayings of Trinidad and Tobago, and the Caribbean

By Josanne Leid

ISBN-13: 978-1500436384
ISBN-10: 1500436380

TABLE OF CONTENTS

Acknowledgements

There are so many fabulous people who encouraged and aided me while I struggled with this book that the book itself would be incomplete without mentioning them: Thank you to the Great Almighty for sending the right people my way; my mother, Frances Romero-Leid, for being so patient with me as I asked her to look at yet another draft -and for putting up with me in general; Aunty Jenny who advised me to change the layout; my friends: Neisha Manickchand, Katrin Callendar and Melissa Mendonça who edited as best they could; my handsome husband Ramoul who basically ordered me to stop messing around and finish the book already; Shaun Riaz especially for his superb and timely drawings; my facebook friends who helped me choose the book cover and to the innumerable others who helped in any small part along the way.

-Thank you

Introduction

The Caribbean like the rest of the 'new' world founded the majority of its population on immigration, indentured labour and slavery. The French, Spanish, Portuguese, British and Dutch took turns colonising at least one island and each insertion of Europeans left an indelible mark on the island's physical and cultural scene. The rulers changed hands often in some cases but their presence is still evident in the agriculture, architecture, education, religion and language of the lands they occupied. When the colonists left, some of the labourers they imported remained, and they as well added to the landscape of the island.

The Chinese, East Indians, and others were shipped in to fill the labour gap when the slave trade was abolished. Like the Europeans, they painted their new homes with their unique way of life, however, the culture that dominates the Caribbean today belongs to the dominant people in colony days- the ex-slaves.

Even as the Europeans ruled, slaves of West African tribal heritage constituted the majority of the population of the Caribbean. A people who were robbed of their freedom, they were consistently tortured until they conformed to their owner's way of life. The slaves adapted to their dependants outwardly in tongue and action but those who could, continued to clandestinely practise what they remembered and passed that knowledge down throughout their imprisonment, even when they were transferred to another owner or land.

In 1783, the *Cédula de Población* authorised French Caribbean residents of Roman Catholic Faith who would swear loyalty to the Spanish Crown, a sizeable land grant depending on different conditions, one of which is the amount of slaves they brought with them. The purpose was to increase inhabitants in the Spanish colony of Trinidad; the result was a heavy infusion of French Creole culture on the tiny island. Even after slavery was abolished the French influence colored the speech and beliefs of the assimilated people and their children. They did not forget their living hell however, and the evil spirits or *jumbies* they warn us about, reflect this. One in particular, Le Diable (Devil) is described as a well dressed white man who makes deals with the living then takes their soul.

Since the abolition of slavery, migration to the Caribbean has increased from countries around the world, and even between Caribbean Islands. Each new resident brings the rituals of their birth home thus augmenting the stock of customs in that island. Add this to the higher percentage of foreign content to local content on information mediums like local television, the internet and literature and it can become difficult over time to remember which practice originated in Caribbean history and which belongs to the heritage of another country.

This book began as a reference of the current culture of the people of the twin isles of Trinidad and Tobago. The information is pre-dominantly from the prevailing heritage-French Creole- but there are a few appearances of the equally dominant influence on the island-East Indian.

While doing the research, the similarity in beliefs between Trinidad and Tobago and its' neighbouring islands was glaringly obvious. Naturally the rest of the Caribbean was appendaged as the shared history has ensured that the superstitions, spirits and sayings showcased are as much theirs as it is of Trinidad and Tobago.

Now, without further ado, I entreat you to turn the page and enjoy a piece of the rich heritage that is uniquely Caribbean; but first, to fully understand what is said, you must know some basic vocabulary...

Vocabulary

Ah- I, of

Am/em- Him, her

Asafetida- A.K.A. the food of the gods, it is a dried gum from a specific herb which has medical value

Bam Bam- Posterior

Blue Soap- A detergent in the form of a blue bar of soap

Bush Bath- A bath taken with various herbs and plants. The most common herbs are: Caile, Congo la-la, Malomae, Sweet Broom, St. John bush, Ruction Bush, Black Sage and Geritout

Buss- Burst open

Cah/Cyah/ Cyar- Can't

Cascadoux- A type of fish

Chook- Stab

Cocoyea- Shards of a Coconut leaf used in crafts like brooms

Corbeau (x) (Fr.)-Raven, Vulture

Crapaud (Fr.) - Toad, Frog

Darg- Dog

Dan- Than

Dat- That

De- The

Dem- Them

Dey- They

Doh- Don't, Doesn't

Donkey eye- Formally known as the seed of the Abrus Precatorius, it is used in making jewellery and as noise-makers in instruments

Eh- Do(es) not

Evil eye- see MAL YEUX

Fuh- For

Go- Will

Goat Mout'- Predicting an outcome- usually negatively- and it comes to pass

'Gouti- Agouti, common rodent

Hops Bread- A type of dinner roll the size of a hamburger bun

Jet beads- Black gems fashioned into jewellery, a very popular present for babies

Jumbie- Spirit, Ghost

Jumbie bead- See DONKEY EYE

Jumbie bird- Owl

Mal Yeux- The look of a jealous or spiteful person intended to harm a person or object A.k.A mal jo

Mas- Annual celebratory event which takes place directly before Lent a.ka. Carnival

Mauby- Caribbean beverage made with spices, sugar and the bark of a particular tree

Mek- Make

Modder- Mother

No/Na/Nuh- Does not

Nyam- Eat

Obeah man- A witchdoctor who usually uses powerful folk magic to harm or control others

Outta- Out of

Pelau- A Trinbago dish comprised of browned rice, pigeon peas and meat mixed together

Pickney- Child

Roti- Trinbago street food made with curry

Trinbago- Shortened form of Trinidad and Tobago

Wake- Christian social gathering that takes place after the death of a person. In rural Caribbean there is a lot of drinking and playing cards

Weh- Which, where

Yampee- Crusty cold found at the corner of the eye when awaking

Yuh- You, your

CHAPTER ONE

Superstitions

How many of us, if millions of dollars were at stake, would not blow on a dice or wear a lucky vest if there was a whiff of a chance that doing so would help us win it? How did we even know what would increase our chances? Few can answer this because the origin of a belief is rarely documented. The belief is usually passed to us through generations of storytelling or through observation until it became a part of our understanding of this world.

The greatest mission of man is to understand the world he lives in. He has come a long way but the earth is almost as dangerous and mysterious now as when homo-sapiens first entered the food chain. In the scope of human history, scientific studies have only recently identified some invisible dangers like airborne diseases and allergens. However, before we became so knowledgeable, our ancestors dealt with their unidentified vulnerability by hypothesizing ways to protect themselves. Without modern day technology they used what was available: a pair of eyes and an observant mind.

The superstitions presented here are the result of those hypotheses. As they have no recorded origin date or creator, they could be from any Caribbean island or not, but they are all known in Trinidad and Tobago and not surprising, some of them even have scientific proof now validating them. The range of knowledge covers warnings and advice for varying situations as well as tips on understanding the natural signs of the world. They have survived by being passed from father to son, mother to daughter until they are well established as a part of the education of the citizens, even if they are not practiced by many.

Part One: Warnings

Caribbean ancestors were a cautious people for good reason. They were charged with ensuring that future generations were not only protected from visible harm but from invisible harm as well. Too many unexplained maladies befell the unsuspecting in their communities. They had survived slavery and knew that hell and demons were real, it was completely reasonable to believe and to pass on to their charges that evil spirits were at work every day to cause them harm, loss, discord, unexpected change and bad luck.

Fortunately, experience or the teachings of their parents armed them with the knowledge necessary to survive the machinations of devils and their duty was to pass on that information. Add that to their responsibility for turning out a well-mannered generation and there is no wonder that a long list of "Don`ts" escaped their mouths on a daily basis- usually followed by a brief beating to emphasize the seriousness of the situation. The following is an articulated version of some of the warnings they shared:

Harm

Don't point a finger at a grave, that finger will start rotting within three days

Spit on the finger twice immediately after pointing to avoid this

Don't exit a house just after hearing the flapping of a goat's ears

Wait a few minutes for the evil to pass then exit

Don't block a doorway in a way that an invisible person cannot pass; if a ghost touches you, you will become ill

Don't let a bird use your hair to makes a nest, you will get a headache

Don't open an umbrella indoors, a *jumbie* will stand under it with you and bring bad luck

Don't eat cheese late at night nor play with your shadow, you will have bad dreams

Don't tell anyone you are leaving at a *wake,* a *jumbie* will overhear you and follow you home

Don't cluck your tongue, you will call a snake

Don't say 'it is your last' anything, it will be a premonition of your death

e.g.: last walk or last drink

Don't write your name in the sand at the beach, the sea will claim your life

Don't place a candle or salt on a doorstep, you will cause the death of a person

Don't write anyone's name on paper and place it in a shoe then wear it, that person will become ill

Don't repeat anyone's name at the end of each verse of the 109th Psalm, the contents of the Psalm will befall him

Don't keep the water used to clean a corpse or let the corpse exit a house anyway other than feet first, its ghost will haunt the house

Don't bury a corpse facing east, instead of resting that ghost will roam for an eternity

Don't hang wind chimes nearby, tinkling chimes attract spirits

Don't allow lizards in the house, spirits travel on them

Don't pick up coins you find on the road, evil spirits or worries on it will pass to you *Persons experiencing bad luck take* bush baths *with a coin in the tub for the problems to seep into the coin. When dropped at a busy intersection, the luck is being 'sold'. The person who picks it up 'buys' the problems and they are transferred to the buyer.*

Don't walk over someone, especially if it is a female over a male or vice versa, you will pass your illnesses or misfortunes to them

Loss

Don't take out the trash or sweep the house after 6 at night, you will remove the wealth from your house

Don't eat the *Cascadoux* fish if you intend to die in a country other than Trinidad and Tobago, no matter where you roam you will end your days in the twin isles

Don't let a woman cut her hair too short, she will lose her wisdom

Don't put your handbag on the floor, you will never have money

Don't do laundry on the first day of the year, a member of your family will be washed away (die)

Change

Don't speak ill of what is yet to happen, your words will make it true a.k.a. *goat-mouth*

Don't bathe in the sea on Good Friday, you will turn into a fish

Don't have sex in a car, the vehicle will develop problems afterward

Don't sweep over someone's feet, that person will never marry

Don't let a straight haired barber cut your hair if you want curly hair

The texture of hair of the barber will determine the texture you will get

Discord

Don't sew on yourself (e.g. a button), others will speak ill of you

Don't pass a knife or hot pepper to anyone, you will have an argument with that person

Don't spill salt, your partner and you will quarrel

Don't place two knives across each other, you will argue with your partner

Don't let a post pass between you and your partner, the relationship will end

Don't put your wedding ring on your engagement finger, it will affect your marriage

Bad Luck

Not completing any of these tasks will automatically entitle you to bad luck therefore:

Don't give someone a lamp that you have used

Don't cut your hair or trim your nails on odd days like Tuesday, Thursday or Saturday

Don't drink lime juice after 12 noon

Don't eat meat of a black pig

Don't hang clothes upside down to dry nor inside out in the closet

Don't hold your head with both hands

Part Two: Advice

Like any benevolent parent, the forebears of the Caribbean have the best interest of their descendants at heart. They have determined that performing certain actions guarantee the attraction of good luck and were determined to pass on that vast knowledge. Not only does that wisdom involve tips on how to prosper in life but also how to protect oneself from physical and ethereal harm, the steps to ensure a healthy baby and directions on producing a good crop. With many years' worth of experience and education as their guide, the following are some of the sage words that have passed their lips to advise us on a daily basis:

Protection

To ward off spirits from entering your home through traveling food, place a hot pepper in the food

To prevent spirits from entering your home with you at night, turn your back to the inside of the house when opening the door and say 'goodnight' loud enough so that any spirits that have followed you home can hear and that spirit will leave

To scare a *jumbie* you suspect is following you, turn your clothes inside out

To keep a *jumbie* at bay, light a match or always keep a matchstick behind your ear when going out at night as a warning

To ensure evil spirits stay away, place *jumbie beads* in kerosene lamps around the house

To see a spirit, put *yampee* from a dog's eye into yours

To avoid seeing the ghost of a recently deceased in a mirror, cover the mirrors in the house with black cloth until after they are buried

To get rid of an unwanted visitor, turn a broom upside down in a corner of the house

To avoid injuring yourself if you are prone to accidents with tools, mark a cross with your fingers on the tool before using it

To protect against dew, *mal yeux* and insincere friendships, wear an amulet of crushed garlic

To protect animals from the *evil eye*, paint blue spots on their forehead and tie black ribbons around their horns or charms around their neck

To protect yourself against a malicious tongue, write the name of that person on a piece of paper, attach it to a Mother in Law's tongue plant (Sansevieria trifasciata) and leave it until it starts to shake

To ensure a *jumbie* does not sleep in your bed while you are out, place a pillow across the bed

To make a *jumbie* disappear, repeat the 'I believe in one God' prayer

To keep *jumbies* from entering your house, close all windows and doors when a funeral procession is passing

Prosperity

To always have food in the house put bread soaked in water on the doorstep and keep at least one lump of coal under the table

To always have money, place corn and a piece of *hops bread* near your money or keep a *donkey-eye* in your wallet

To erase bad luck, bathe with *blue soap* or have a *bush bath* every now and then

To maintain your luck, wash food containers before returning them to their owners

In the New Year:

Avoid cleaning the house on New Year's Day, good fortune will be swept away

Clean the house thoroughly on Old Years to clean out any problems from the old year

Actions on New Year's Day sets the tone for the rest of the year

E.g. empty cupboard means scarcity for that year

Eating black-eyed peas on New Year's Day will attract good luck

Produce

To protect harvest from withering via the *evil eye*, place a chamber pot or blue bottle or, white bottle with blue spots painted on them upside down on a stick in the middle of the crop's field

To get an early crop of pineapple, dig a hole by making one stroke with a fork while planting- *The amount of strokes used to dig the hole is the amount of years the crop will take to mature*

To make the cassava crop sweeter, drink honey before planting

To make a barren breadfruit tree bear fruit, chop off some branches- *This method is scientifically proven to redistribute nutrients*

To avoid a disastrous corn crop, eat before planting

Don't pick fruits after 6 p.m., the tree is sleeping

To change a tree from male to female for reproduction, hammer a rusty nail into it- *Scientists believe that nails made with zinc inject a chemical to make this occur*

To ensure young fruits grow to maturity, avoid pointing at them

To avoid bad luck, destroy a plantain sucker which shoots to the west

To avoid a disappointing harvest, stand while planting crops

Pregnancy

To have an easy birth, eat a lot of okras/ochroes leading up to the birthing to make the birth canal moist and slimy for the baby to slip through easily

To avoid an overly plump baby, reduce the amount of ice eaten during pregnancy

To have a fair skinned child, drink a lot of milk during pregnancy, and chocolate milk to get a dark skinned baby

To eliminate the chances of your baby being born with a birthmark in the shape of a denied food, satisfy food cravings immediately. However, eating too much of one food also, bears a baby with a mark in the shape of that food. To avoid this the mother should gently massage her bottom if the craving cannot be satisfied.

Beware of horse whip snakes as they are attracted to and will sting a pregnant woman with its tail

To 'smoke out' any evil in the house before the baby arrives, mix solid bits of *asafetida*, incense and dried orange peel in a container and light it afire before carrying it throughout the house

To abort a baby, drink a hot Guinness no later than the morning after intercourse

Food made by the pregnant cook is not up to her usual standards, she will either be better or worse depending on the baby

To ensure a healthy baby, do not look at or let the rays of a full moon touch you while pregnant

To avoid a long labor, the mother should not cross her legs during pregnancy

Progeny

Bury the birth chord of the new born at the foot of a prolific fruit tree to ensure the fertility of the child as an adult. *Burying the chord beneath any tree ensures black magic practitioners are unable to use this part of the body to control the child*

Cover the top of the baby's head (fontanelle) at all times when leaving the house as a spirit can enter from there

To cure a baby's hiccoughs, take a thread from its clothing and stick it to the child's forehead with the mother's saliva

To ensure a baby does not grow up stammering, avoid

tickling the child

A baby that cuts the two upper teeth first brings infertility to the parents

Children must not stand under an umbrella at home nor turn a calabash on its head, their growth would be stunted

To protect the baby from harm:

Pin a sachet of indigo and *asafetida* on the babe's vest and keep an open bible with a pair of scissors across the bible nearby

Hang pieces of cacti or a cross marked with indigo blue over the window to prevent evil spirits from entering the baby's room

Ensure the baby wears *jumbie* or *jet beads* to ward off disease and *mal yeux*

Bathe babies often with *blue soap* to keep away disease

Pass a coin around the child 5 times then throw it away just before the babe is introduced to strangers in order to avoid them harming the child

Pass the baby over the coffin of a relative so that ghost will not harass the baby

To protect the baby from harmful forces, keep the infant in the house until it is christened

Physical Well Being

To reduce severe aches wrap a knife in bay leaf and bandage it over a tender or injured spot

To keep arthritis away, wrap a copper wire around your wrists

To ensure the length of a menstrual cycle lasts only three days, the initiate must thread a palm leaf around the fingers of her right hand and then cut the leaf between her fingers

To end a quarrel, spill salt on the floor

To stop your ears from ringing when someone is talking about you, call the name of the person you think is the culprit

Part Three: Interpreting Signs and Symbols

In addition to great wisdom on how to avoid harm and loss and how to attract prosperity, the ancients were very knowledgeable on the meanings of natural phenomenon. So sharp and analytical was their mind that they effortlessly deciphered the co-relation between one event and a deceptively irrelevant outcome. Most of their interpretations focused on the preoccupations of humanity such as money, good and bad tidings. The following are a few of the more famous translations:

Money

A brown spider or brown grasshopper in the house means money will soon arrive

The dominant (right) palm of your hand itching means money will be received soon

The other (left) palm of your hand itching means you will have unexpected expenses soon

A green grasshopper in the house means money will be spent soon

Good Tidings

Pigeon feces on anything means good luck to the owner of the item

A person appearing just after being talked about will live long into their dotage

A man in a relationship who is suddenly eating a lot means his girlfriend or wife is pregnant

A butterfly in a house means good luck is on its way

A *cocoyea* broom symbolizes peace and goodwill

The right eye suddenly "jumping" means you will see someone you have not seen in a long time

A live chicken shaking itself in front of someone means that person will soon get a gift

Complete silence for a moment means angels are passing by

Someone with a gap between their front teeth or who was once bow legged as a child, are great bed partners

The white of an egg forming a cathedral in a glass of water on Good Friday means a wedding is on its way

Mistakenly laying an extra place at the table means a visitor will arrive before the end of the meal

A bird flying into the house means a visitor is on its way

The sole of your foot itching means you will soon take a long journey

Two spoons in one serving dish means a wedding will take place

Lightening flashing means all the evil in the air is being destroyed

Bad Tidings

Food falling before reaching your mouth means either, someone is envious of something you possess and will soon try to take it, or a *jumbie* is desirous of eating with you. *To keep your possession, quickly put the food in your mouth no matter where it has fallen*

A cock crowing at the door means someone inside the house will die shortly

A black bird outside your window means someone you know will die soon

A widow's peak on a forehead indicates she will bury three husbands before her

Ringing ears means someone is talking ill about you

A bit tongue means someone is speaking ill about you or you said something you weren't supposed to say

An owl hooting near your house means harm or death will occur to someone close to you. *To chase away the owl: ignite a flame and hold a needle or nail over it until it gets hot. The heat is magically transferred to the owl and it flies away*

The loud sound of something heavy dropping on your slanted roof without rolling means someone close to you will die

A change in menses from regular to irregular while faithful to one person means he is cheating on you

A second toe longer than the big toe on a woman means she is going to beat or rule her husband

A dog barking incessantly when nothing is around means it is seeing a spirit

A howling dog means death is eminent

Speaking a name mistakenly in conversation means that person is talking about you

Rain and sunshine at the same time means a devil is getting married behind a church or he and his wife are fighting for a hambone

Part of your dress hem turned up means somebody is speaking ill about you

Sneezing means your spirit is trying to escape your body- *so cover your mouth*

Unable to move your body on awaking means your spirit has yet to return from its night travels

Someone with a mole on their lip is a liar and cheat

A live frog with its mouth padlocked on your doorstep means the *Obeah man* will harm you if you do not change your ways

The white of an egg forming a coffin in a glass of water on Good Friday means death is short to follow

A jumping eye means either you will receive bad news, or rain will fall shortly

A cat washing its face with its paw means rain will fall soon

Accepting scissors of steel from a friend brings the friendship to an untimely end

CHAPTER TWO

Spirits

Jumbie, Jack O' Lantern, Baku and Duppy all mean one thing in the Caribbean- Spirit. In Trinidad and Tobago and the majority of the Caribbean islands, the *jumbie* is malevolent and aims to haunt and harm the living. In Jamaica, Antigua and Barbuda, Barbados and Guyana the temperament of the Duppy and Baku depends on the character of the body it once inhabited. Meanwhile the Jack O' Lantern is mischievous as it shines a light to lead travelers astray in the dark. No matter the type of spirit, the popular supernatural beings that roam each island are concentrated in wooded and lonely areas.

Forests are famously filled with Spirits and their familiars. Animals and plants with characteristics of a *jumbie,* that is, terrifying and treacherous, are named after them. An owl is commonly called a *Jumbie Bird* and is associated with death and destruction probably because it flies at night, the time when evil spirits supposedly roam. Black or dark hued animals are also eyed suspiciously as shape shifting spirits prefer those shades. The famous haunts of the spirits are the: Neem, Calabash and Mango trees. The Silk Cotton tree however is the preferred resting place of truly evil spirits. Brave souls who are forced to cut these trees down must first make peace offerings in the form of food or drink at the base of that tree to avoid angering the residing *jumbie.*

The most famous Silk Cotton Tree is the Castle of the Devil. Said to be located in the deep forests of Trinidad and Tobago, it is fabled that a powerful devil called Bazil was tricked into entering the altered tree by a wily carpenter who had carved seven rooms one on top of the other inside so the devil could not escape. Bazil has not lost his powers though and is known to use minions in his stead. He often exchanges his power for obedience from black magic practitioners who seek him out.

The spirits represented in this section reflect some of the migrations resulting from our various colonisations. Just like the various names for 'spirit', the name of the spirits will be different from island to island. Despite this, their character is recognized in the similarity of their folk-tale.

La Diablesse

Translated as 'female devil' from French, La Diablesse was born human but her dealings with the devil have made her a malicious shape-shifting spirit. Her face is now either dreadfully distorted in a ghastly gray hue with fierce fangs or it is a human skull, but it is always hidden by a large straw hat.

To those under her spell, she appears beautiful, in whatever form the victim thinks is beautiful. She cannot spell herself completely though so under her long- sometimes traditional French creole- dress, one cow's hoof reveals her identity.

Her victims of preference are men of wealth and/or social standing and she is often spotted loitering outside social gatherings, along lonely roads, cemeteries and near cross roads. Those accepting her offer to walk with her are led off the path and lured to their death at a Silk Cotton Tree or over a cliff or, if she feels lenient, she would simply transform into a huge hog and disappear from sight leaving him lost.

There are accounts of people passing her at one size, then, looking back when they hear footsteps following them, realize she has grown bigger in size each time they turn around. She will eventually give chase taunting and laughing at her victim until he reaches home, then through the window will laugh and say 'ou tini bonheur' (you are lucky) and disappear.

She is also believed to be behind the little child sitting by the road crying. When her victim stops to inquire the cause, the child will cry that she is lost and beg to be lifted. When the child is picked up to be carried to the address given, the victim is told the house is always just a little further than was previously said. At the same time, the weight of the child becomes heavier and heavier with each step. When the victim realizes the situation he hears La Diablesse cackle as he flees.

To make her disappear, find two sticks and position them like a cross in front of her. As sticks are not always present when you need them, its best to: avoid beautiful ladies with long dresses; call the police if you find a child crying at the side of the road; and if someone following you has gotten taller the first time you turn around- run!

Phantom

A.K.A: Moon gazer

Standing over 40 feet tall, the Phantom straddles a crossroad while staring silently up at the moon. As people or cars approach, he snaps his legs shut, squeezing them to death. Their only warning is a shrill, spine-tingling whistle he emits before his assault.

To avoid being squashed, look up before passing through two tall 'poles' near the road to ensure they aren't legs. If they are legs, pass around it.

Buck

Originating from Guyana, this little man-like being with sharp teeth and long claws has been spotted in other Caribbean countries. Believed to be small enough to fit inside a glass jar, it can be controlled effortlessly through food.

It is said that when captured, the Buck grants it's jailor as many wishes as long as it is fed regularly with a diet that includes milk. Miss a meal and it easily escapes to viciously enact revenge on its captor.

So, keep a large supply of food close by or else keep away from Buck

Mama D'leau

A.K.A: Mother of the River; Water Mooma; Fairy maid; Cribeau

A rumored lover of Papa Bois, Mama D'leau is the protector and healer of all river animals. She often appears as a beautiful woman seated on a rock at the river's edge, or at water wheels combing her long golden hair with a golden comb.

When angered each strand of her hair turns into a serpent and shining scales cover her body. From her waist downwards the scales twist into coils like an anaconda and her tongue becomes forked.

In Grenada she wears a golden crown and if you take possession of the crown you will receive untold riches, but, she will follow you to the end of the earth until it is returned.

To escape her, turn your left shoe upside down and walk backwards until you reach home. If pursued on land, zigzag, as she only moves in a straight line.

Saapin

From East Indian lore, this beautiful being has a tattoo of a cobra along its spinal chord or thigh, and can have up to seven partners in one lifetime.

The Saapin behaves and looks human until certain times of the year. At that time and only at midnight when the moon is full, the image on its body comes alive and it turns into a half-snake- upper body human, lower body snake. It bites its mate while they sleep thus marking them for death. Soon after their mate dies by 'accident' by a different means so no one would suspect her.

To placate the snake spirit, perform a naag pooja (snake worship ceremony).

Loup Garou

Courtesy of the French influence, Loup Garou means 'a man who turns into a wolf'. In the Caribbean version, the beast often appears with a chain around its neck and it can walk on two feet. Some islanders believe the Loup Garou can be identified during the day as a very hairy person with bruised palms and knees (because the devil rides them at night).

Legend says that the person who sheds the blood of a Loup Garou forces it to change to its human form and reveal its identity. As punishment, that person becomes a Loup Garou for one hundred and one days. If that person tells anyone, she or he will remain a Loup Garou forever; otherwise, will return to human form permanently after penance.

To see a Loup Garou in its shifted form, put the *yampee* from a dog in your own eye and look through a keyhole at midnight, then stay away from it.

Papa Bois

A.K.A: Maitre Bois; Daddy Bouchon

Hairy, short and powerful looking, this shape shifting spirit prefers to appear with the upper body of a man and the lower body of a beast with hooves for feet and small horns protruding from his forehead.

Some believe he was once a hunter who disappeared into the forest to make amends by protecting and tending the animals he'd once preyed on. Hunters who hear a horn blown in the deep forest know to beware; Papa Bois has spotted them and is warning his wards.

Depending on his mood that day, he will either cause his enemies to become lost in the forest or send them to their doom. He does this by changing into the animal that is hunted and leading them deep into the untamed woods. Several days later, if he allows it, they will be found half dead with hunger and exhaustion, a stone's throw away from a well-beaten path which somehow they were unable to find.

If you encounter Papa Bois, hold his gaze while saying prayers in Spanish (oraciones) and walk backwards away from him. He will not be able to move, and at a safe distance, run. Afterward, it is advised not to enter a forest to hunt because he will be waiting.

Soucouyant

A.K.A: Ole Hige/ Old Hag/ Wangla Lady

Depicted as a grumpy, unsociable old woman with red where the whites of the eyes should be, she sheds her human skin at midnight to feed on the blood of the humans she has entranced to sleep deeply.

She can fit through any sized hole and the only evidence of the visit is the blue-black marks that remain on the sucked parts of the victim's body on awaking. However, if too much blood is drawn, the victim will either turn into a Soucouyant or else die and the Soucouyant will keep their skin.

The Soucouyant`s true form is a ball of fire seen flying across the night sky either in search of its next victim or heading to the Silk Cotton Tree to barter some of its victim's blood for favours and powers from Bazil, the devil who resides there.

There are three ways to prove someone is a Soucouyant:

1. She appears as if she is floating off the ground when viewed from between your legs

2. She changes direction when she sees a cross

3. She picks up a spilled heap of rice grain by grain

To protect yourself while you sleep, make a circle with chalk or salt on the floor around your bed and the Soucouyant cannot cross. Another method is to scatter rice around your bed to delay the creature until dawn breaks, when it is compelled to locate its skin.

To destroy it, find its human skin, normally hidden under a mortar in the Soucouyant's bedroom, and sprinkle salt or pepper in it. When the skin is put on, it will burn the Soucouyant to death.

Cocoya

Cousin of the Soucouyant, this aged female creature also appears as a ball of fire and has a deep fear of the cross. However, the Cocoya is joyous and loves to sing. Her meal of choice is the meat of the males she lures to her house. Interestingly though, she would do anything to help a fellow female.

To destroy her, expose her to sunlight. Sunlight makes her shrivel up and blow away

Dee Baba

An estate manager who once lived almost a century ago at a sugar estate in Debe, Trinidad, it is said Dee Baba's spirit is seen now between midnight and the early mornings in rural Trinidad.

He appears as either a white man on a black horse, or as a black rooster or black dog. Farmers leave offerings to him hoping to reap abundant harvest and for protection of themselves and their property from illness, theft and the *evil eye*. Ceasing his offerings often results in loss of his protection and eventually, harm.

Leave a little gift at an impromptu shrine for him if you don't want his ire.

Gang Gang Sarah

A.K.A The witch from Golden Lane

Legend says one stormy night in the 18th century she was blown from Africa to Tobago and landed in Les Coteaux.

She journeyed to Golden Lane where her family had been transported before her, and she became the village midwife, which earned her the name of Gang Gang. She eventually married but when her husband died she became lonely and wanted to return to Africa.

Not realizing she'd eaten enough salt to destroy her spiritual strength and her ability to fly, she leapt off the tallest Silk Cotton Tree in Culloden and fell to her death. Her descendants allow visitors to her unmarked grave beside her husband's however, some believe witches never stay buried...

Douen

A.K.A: Duaine; Bush Dai Dai; Douenne

Believed to be a child who died before being christened, it is
reborn as a sexless creature with backward facing feet and
never taller than three feet high. Its featureless face is always

hidden by a huge mushroom-shaped straw hat and it communicates with a sound like 'Whoop, Whoop!'

Douennes stay in packs and haunt forested and lonely places. They like to play near water sources like rivers, and to lure children deep into the forest to play with them. They get their victim's name by overhearing it. They then use it to draw the child further and further into the forest until the child becomes lost, confused and afraid. One source revealed a child was found caged after such an episode.

Children are favoured but not their only prey. A darker end to one of their games is to lure their victim into a deep pool where she or he sinks to the bottom. The only way known to make them leave you alone is to shout profanities at them. To avoid their notice, it is best to never shout a person's name after dark in open places.

In rural areas of the Caribbean, a child often has two names: official and home name to confuse spirits and protect him or her from harm.

Raakha

Told to us by our East Indian heritage, this new born baby of unsuspecting parents is described as being dark, with a high sloping forehead, long hair, two protruding teeth on upper and lower jaw and long finger and toe nails.

On birth, its purpose is to kill it`s mother. If the first attempt fails, it swiftly escapes and will cause dissention in the neighborhood until it fulfills its goal.

The person delivering the baby is obligated to destroy it as soon as it comes out the mother. Otherwise wait it out, a Raakha does not live beyond a few days.

Mama Malade

She is the spirit of a woman who died in childbirth. She roams at night searching for the spirit of people she wants to take. She lures unsuspecting victims by making the sound of a child crying outside their window. Anyone who investigates is never seen from again.....

La Gahoo

A.K.A: Li Gahoo

A relative of the Loup Garou, this spirit has the ability to shift into animal form and has been seen previously as a creature similar to a centaur. However, he favours the shape of a robust man with a coffin for a head. Atop the coffin, three candles stand with flickering flames.

He is often heard before seen, as long loose ends of the heavy iron chain around his waist drag along the road. Some say he feeds on humans but he is widely known to suck the blood of livestock like cows and goats. His main amusement is to scare others by changing his size at will no matter his current form.

To kill a La Gahoo, beat the creature with a stick anointed with holy water and holy oil for nine days. It changes to other beasts throughout the ordeal before disappearing into mist

CHAPTER THREE

Sayings

English is the first official language of many Caribbean islands but not everything said by those Caribbean people can be translated literally into English. Sarcasm and the double entendre saturate our speech to the point where we can confuse even ourselves much less non-natives. One example of this is in our pet names for each other. If someone is tall their own friends christen them 'shorty.' If they are obese, their family names them 'slim'. It is no wonder some of our own proverbs can mean something completely outside of what it should suggest.

This innate contrariness started being documented in colonial days in Trinidad and Tobago as evidenced by the remains of early musical creations like Calypso. Calypso being the commentary of current society, it is unsurprisingly not appreciated by those in authority. The only way not to end up in jail or worse was to hide the meaning with other words.

The sayings compiled in the following pages cannot be taken at face value. To complicate matters further, they can have different meanings in different settings. One example is: *Little axe does cut down big tree.* Depending on the context, the saying can mean: the smallest action can have dire consequences or small people can accomplish great things.

To reduce confusion only one translation has been provided below most statements, however, as several different sayings can mean the same thing, each of those saying are shown on the same line and separated by semi- colons.

The statements presented are a mix of wise and common phrases used unconsciously in everyday dialogue. Their original creole format has been retained so that the local parlance is fully appreciated and that there is no loss in translation. Turn the page and be surrounded by the soothing sounds and hilarious creativity of Caribbean Sayings.

Nature

Doh count egg in fowl bottom

Don't consider or use something until you have it in your possession, e.g. money

Peas *doh* bear corn; Goat *doh* make sheep; Guinea hen *doh* make ram goat

Offspring are just like their parents in character and actions

The higher the plum tree the riper the plum

The more difficult it is to attain a goal, the sweeter the victory will be

White dog *doh* eat white dog

Those of the same ilk will always look out for each other

If *yuh* leave cocoa in *de* sun, look out for rain

Be wary if you have something to hide

D eyes of master fatten *d* calf;

Supervision always yields better performance

Get cage before *yuh* get bird

*Make sure you can support yourself or can afford a house before
you get married*

No gully no deh to t'row bad fam'ly

No matter the troubles, family always sticks together

Where molasses is, fly must be

Those of the same ilk are never far apart

Play dead to catch *corbeaux*

Pretend ignorance to later expose a situation

Same t`ing in snake head in bow stick head

Everyone wants to get the better of the other one

People *doh* t'row stone at mango tree that *doh* bear fruit

It's human nature to criticise successful people

Beg water never boil cow skin

When you get what you ask for, it is never enough

Yuh cyar chook down God with bamboo

God doesn't exist to fulfill your whims

Two bo-rat *cyah* live in one hole

Two strong characters cannot live peacefully together

Makin' track *fuh* 'gouti to run

Experiencing hardships to pioneer something and others afterwards easily reap your rewards

What sweet in goat mout' sour in he *bam bam*

Pleasure has consequences

What is joke *fuh* schoolboy is deat` *fuh crapaud*

Every action affects others, what is good for you could be bad for someone else

Don't sit down on river stone and talk river

Don't gossip

Only two jack-ass should bray at *d* same time

Let the arguers continue uninterrupted until they can calm down to be sensible

Bush have ears

Someone is always listening

Dat doh change *d* price *ah* cocoa
It does not change a thing

Ah hear better cock *dan* you crow (and still end up in the *pelau*)
Someone more qualified than you has tried and failed

When cock get teet'
It will never happen

Give *darg* enough rope it ah hang itself
Let the person continue talking

Cockroach have no right in fowl party; Rock 'tone nuh have calling
a egg party
That person does not belong here

Monkey know which tree to climb an' which fruit in season; Hog
know wha' tree tuh rub hi skin 'pan
Bullies know which person to harass and when to do it

Bend *de* tree when it start to grow
Train the child when s/he is young

Every bara hog gat 'e Saturday

Misfortunes happen to everybody eventually

Monkey *doh* see he own tail

People don't acknowledge their own faults but are hasty to judge others

Fisherman *doh* say he fish rotten

Someone trying to sell you something will never admit to its flaws

Kitchen dresser brock down marga *darg* a larf

One person's misfortune is another's good luck

Yuh make chile but *yuh doh* make *dey* mind

Train your child all you like but it's their choice how they behave

When rain fall, sheep and goat does have to mix

When times bad, everybody suffer together

Robber pocket have no bottom

Can't change the nature of a person

Pickney a *nyam* muma but muma na *nyam pickney*

Mothers will always love their children no matter what they do.

Personal Affairs

Never interfere wi' man and woman *weh* a sleep in one bed

Don't meddle in someone else's family business because they will reap the consequences

Penny-wise, pound-foolish

Doing something small now would prevent much more trouble later

Empty bag *cyar* stand

Without your own values, you follow others' possibly to your detriment

Gopaul luck is no' Seepaul luck

What works for one person doesn't work for someone else

Do so *eh* like so

People don't like when their malicious treatment of others is reciprocated

What is to is must is

What will be, will be

Food

Before *darg* gone wit'out supper he *nyam* raw corn-flour
When times are bad, make do with what you have

Wrapped up like a *roti*
Tightly packaged

Dem who encourage *yuh fuh* buy big belly horse no *dem* why ah
help you feed am;
Friends will take yuh but dey doh bring yuh back
*People who you think are your friends will put you in a bad situation
and not help you out of it*

Every bread has its cheese
There is someone made for everyone on this earth

What *dey* give you to rub, you eat
You believe anything

Bad family no bitter cassava; Bitter cassava pisen you
Don't throw your family away even if they are bad to you

Water more than flour, 'tory yella
Falling on hard times

All food good to eat but all talk en good to talk; Talk half lef' half
Don't say everything that comes to mind

Yuh cookin' wit' gas; Yuh on like boil corn
Doing it correctly

Hurry-Hurry cook does bu'n down kitchen
Rushing to complete a task causes many errors

Eat *d* bread that *d* devil knead
To have a difficult life

Take wit' a pinch a salt
Don't believe everything said

Feed wit' a long spoon
Be wary of a person

Corbeau cyar eat sponge cake
Uncomfortable out of your class

Yuh cyah make love on hungry belly
Money makes a relationship last

The dog that brings a bone carries a bone
Persons who relate gossip to you will gossip about you

Champagne taste with *mauby* pocket
Wanting an expensive lifestyle but not having the money to achieve it

Anatomy

All shine/skin teet' no good laugh

Those who you think are your friends may be laughing at you

Jigger feet clear *d* way, rock stone coming down

Be careful if you are vulnerable

What hu't eye, does *mek* nose run

What affects one family member, affects the other

Teet' and tongue does have to meet one day

The best of friends will fall out eventually

Doh le' yuh right han' know wha' yuh lef' han' doing

Don't tell anyone what you are doing until it is done if you want it to be accomplished

Heat in *yuh* tail but yuh whistling

Pretend to be okay but you are hurting

Go blow *yuh* nose whey tuh ketch *yuh* cold

Where you found trouble, go there for sympathy

Mouth open 'tory jump out

Once you start talking, you unwittingly confess everything

Never see come see

Over curious gathering at a scene

One eye man a king a blind eye country

Some leaders are barely better off to lead than their subjects

What ears hear, tongue should know

Think before speaking

Co-operation

Drop by drop does full bucket
Little by little things get done

It take two hands (to clap)
To achieve anything you need help

Plenty han' *mek* work light
More people working together means the work finishes faster

It take two fingers to kill louse
Man and wife must stick together

Rub *meh* belly ah scratch *yuh* back
If you help me, I will help you

Punishment

One/99 day(s) *fuh* t'ief one day for police; One day one day
congotay

Sooner or later there will be a day of reckoning

Who *doh* hear does feel; Chile *dat doh* hear *modder* does drink tea
wit'out sugar

If you don't pay attention, you will be punished

It good for *yuh*

You had it coming

Yuh coo-coo cook

You're in serious trouble

D change from *d* dollar does cause *d* noise

Back-chat makes trouble

Crapaud smoke *yuh* pipe

Now you're in a lot of trouble

Nuh drink ginger tea/ take medicine for other people fever

Don't take punishment for other's problems

Value

Cheap t'ing no good and good t'ing no cheap
Things of value are expensive

What *eh* meet *yuh eh* pass *yuh*
What you don't see, you don't need

Behind back is dog, before face is Mr. Dog
Pretending to know a powerful person when talking to friends

Fuh to be poor nuh crime buh *fuh* nasty is sin
It' okay to be underprivileged but not to behave badly

Howdy and t'anky break no bones
It doesn't hurt to use manners

Troubles

Run from *d jumbie* butt up on *d* coffin

From a bad situation to a worse one

When you in good house, bad house go call *yuh*

Being unfaithful in marriage

Parents gather with rake, children throw away with shovel

*What the parents painstakingly accumulate, their offspring
carelessly waste*

Modder dead, family done

*The mother is the anchor that keeps the family together, without her
the family isn't as close*

If it ain't come out in the wash it *go* come out in the rinse

The truth will come out eventually

Appearances

Yuh know book but not chapter
You never really know a person/situation

It have more in *de* mortar than *de* pestle
There is more to the situation than meets the eye

Man wha' does cuss he *modder*, go beat he wife
Can judge the character of a man from how he treats his mother

Black is white
Anything goes

Bright but not shining
Not too smart

Take a 6 for a 9
To be hoodwinked

You *cyar* be ugly and bad lucky
Impossible to have two negatives against you at same time

Cut *yuh* style to suit *yuh* clothes; Measure *yuh* waist before you go a
tailor shop; Cut *yuh* suit according to *yuh* clot'

Live within your means

Never hang *yuh* hat where *yuh* han' *cyah* reach

Don't exceed your limit

Who *d* cap fit, pull *de* string

Who fits the description, is responsible

Come visit and come live with me is two different t'ings

Your mate's true character is revealed only after you move in

Comparison

Like chalk and cheese
Very different

Feel like a bite up shillin'
To feel overjoyed

Like it goin' outta style
Behaving as if there is no tomorrow

Like spinning top in mud
Going nowhere

Like crab in barrel
Climbing over each other to get to top but never will

Like a wet fowl
A frizzled appearance

Like lickin' cork
Doing well

Pass meh like ah exam
Passed by without a greeting

Like a Wednesday
Always in the middle of something

Like bim and bam
Always together

Like cat and dog
Always fighting

Like s/he swallow a dictionary
Verbose

Cool like Gokool
Worry free

Like money in *d* bank
Guaranteed

Cold like dog nose

Describes anything that is supposed to be hot but is not

E.g. food

Licks like fire/peas

Continuous beating/ tromping of a person

Happy like pappy

Very happy

Expressions

Ah never see more!

How rude!

Choo pool!

To hell with you!

Fuh so!

A plenty!

Jeez-an'-ages; Come nah man

Oh gosh!

A'ieu (ah-yo) Pancho!

Let's go!

Papa yo; Oui Papa!

Well, well (expression of surprise or agreement)

Ah go dance at *yuh* wedding (an' bongo at yuh wake)

Expression of thanks meaning: to reciprocate your kindness, I will rejoice in your good times and cry in your bad times

• • •

Cool *yuh* herbs
Relax!

Wha' trouble/ *d'* jail is dis!
What the hell

But how you mean
Well of course

Call *dat* George
It's over

Doh make joke
Really?

Dat is joke…
That is nothing compared to what I am going to say next

We go pick up
See you later

Yuh go de'd like a semp with two foot in *d* air
A curse said in anger which hopes an ugly death on the person

Trinbago verbs

To buss *de* mark

To expose all the gory details of a secret

To buss a lime

To start a gathering or party

To break biche; L'école biche

To skip school

To ban' yuh belly

To be more economical in hard times

To buy cat in bag

To accept something without verifying it e.g. information/products

To get blank/brace

To be snubbed when trying to attract someone

To be a Bobolee

To be taken advantaged of/ to be a fool

To be Bazodi

To be confused/ in love

To have no broughtupcy

To have no manners

To try a t'ing

To attempt when all odds are against it

To coskel

To dress or adorn self outrageously e.g. with too bright coulours

Can be used as a noun

To digs out/ to dust it

To leave hurriedly

To feel a-how

To feel out of sorts

To eat parrot bottom

To talk too much

To dirty my/person's waters

To make life difficult for me/that person

Lagniappe

A little something extra

Fresh water Yankee

Person who speaks with an American accent even though visited there a short time

…is people too

We are all equal

Behind God's back; Quite-o quite-o

Very far place; In the middle of no-where

Can't play sailor *mas* an' 'fraid powder

Before you enter a situation, make sure you are the right person for the task

Beat *de* iron while it hot

Act while the moment is fresh

Cote ci cote la

A long drawn out explanation

Monday could fall on a Sunday; Sunday could fall on a Tuesday
Totally oblivious of surroundings and events

Catch yuhself
Watch what you say

Come good
Try your best

Everyday bucket a go a well one day it bottom ah stap dey
Taking without returning eventually ends the relationship

When fire ketch yah brudder board, wet yours
Be cognizant of events around you so you are prepared when disaster strikes

When man *na* get luck, wet paper cut him
An unlucky person is very unlucky

If *yuh cah* catch mammy, catch pappy
If you can't get through one way, try another way

Ole fire sticks easy to catch
Ex-lovers can easily reunite

Dat and God face you'll never see

You're not going to see whatever it is you want to see

Put that in yuh pipe an' smoke it

A polite way to say 'shove it where the sun don't shine'

After freeness is penis

When you think someone is helping out of the goodness of their hearts, in reality they want something in return, often what you don't want to give

Appendix

Activity One

How well do you know your Caribbean Sayings? Below is a list of proverbs, if you think you know their meaning and wish to share your answers, write on Myths and Maxims wall on Facebook. Are you ready? Setty? Go!

Ratta tongue ah sell I he

Not for the want ah tongue meh cow cant tark

When you see dag a pass wit hi harf rope ah I neck let it guh weh yah guh

De same day green bush frop a water nuh de same day yah rotten

Monkey eye deep all about

Goat dung bin want to roll loud before wind blow

If pee nuh bin hot fowl woulda pee

Bull old caca daub hi tail

Monkey know how tuh measure he own tail

Ants take over all the grease

Horses for courses

Horse never too lazy to carry he own oars

Cane no grow like grass

Is trouble make monkey eat pepper

Muddy water could wash copper

Jail eh make to ripen fig

Sparrow does fly high but must come down low to sleep

Evening sun can't dry blanket

Who in d kitchen does feel d heat

One eye dag nah ramp a sand

Spit in sky go fall back in your eye

Full belly man does tell hungry belly man 'keep heart'

Ashes cold pappy lay down

Common sense make before book sense

Is not the man who shit in d road does remember, is d man who mash it

Liars have no memory

What you can hide from a t'ief you can't hide from a liar

No t'ief like to see another t'ief basket full

Beg from beggar never grow rich

T'ief from t'ief make God laugh

Tompi buy trouble, job cyar cure 'em

Bakra work never done

Moon does run till day catch it

Make sure better cock sure

Shroud eh have pocket

Bambye you go c am

Laugh an' cry live in d same house

Two wrongs don't make a right

Scornful dog does eat from dutty calabash

Bundle wood have to loose before it tie good
Man dead, grass grow in he door/mouth

Activity 2

For this activity match the answer with their description. Good Luck.

Answers:

Mermen; Castle of the Devil; Bois du Soleil; Fairy maids

Description:

A woodsman spirit of the forest not as popular as Papa Bois

A huge Silk Cotton Tree deep in the forest in which Bazil, the demon of death was imprisoned by a carpenter. The carpenter tricked him to enter the tree in which he carved seven rooms one above the other.

A handsome half man, half fish which lives deep in the sea and can grant a wish.

Maiden of the rivers and waterwheels who mate with mermen.

###

Bibliography:

Ottley, C.R. Legends, True Stories and Old Sayings from Trinidad and Tobago. Port-of-Spain: The College Press, 1962. Print.

Elder, J.D. Ma Rose Point: An Anthology of Rare Legends and Folk Tales from Trinidad and Tobago. Port-of-Spain: National Cultural Council of Trinidad and Tobago, 1972. Print.

Brant, Ed Wynn. "Walk Backward Or You' Coocoo cook." The Trinidad Express 3 Sept. 1972: 26. Print.

Anthony, Michael. Caribbean Folk Tales & Fantasies. Oxford: MacMillan, 2004. Print.

Mills, Therese. "Just hammer in a nail: logic in old beliefs that cannot be written off." The Sunday Guardian 4 Dec. 1966: n. pag. Print.

"Local Legends, folktales and superstitions of Tobago." The Trinidad Guardian 23 Oct. 2010: 43. Print.

Simpson, George E. "Folk Medicine in Trinidad." Journal of American Folklore Oct-Dec. 1962: n.pag. Print.

Miggins, Deborah Moore. The Caribbean Proverbs that raised us. Denver, Colorado: Outskirts Press, 2007. Print.

Baptiste, Rhona. Trini talk- a dictionary of words and proverbs of T&T. n.p: 1994. Print.

Besson, Gerard. Folklore and Legends of Trinidad and Tobago. Port-of-Spain: Paria Publishing, 1989. Print.

Besson, Gerard and Brereton, Bridget. The Book of Trinidad. Port-of-Spain: Paria Publishing, 2010. Print.

Ramsawack, Al. "Nature Trail: Pol-pol Owl Feared by the Highly Superstitious Folk." The Trinidad Guardian, 26 Apr. 1980: 21. Print.

Pierre, Barry V. Verbum Sap. A Tribute to L.O. Inniss. Port-of-Spain. Self-Published, 2000. Print.

Springer, Pearl A.L.A. "Folk Practices in Trinidad & Tobago: Man Peaba Woman Peaba" Caribbean Medical Journal Vol. 40 (1979): 59-60. Print.

Niehoff, Arthur. 'The Spirit world of Trinidad' Shell Trinidad Vol. 5 (n.d): 1.Print.

Seunarine, Lance. Stories me moddha told meh. New York, Trican Book. Nd. Print

Mahabir, Kumar. Indian Caribbean Folklore Spirits. Port of Spain. Chakra Publishing House. 2010. Print.

www.ingramcontent.com/pod-product-compliance
Lightning Source LLC
Chambersburg PA
CBHW050503290526
45786CB00006B/2409